Desert

my guide to earth's habitats

Susan H. Gray

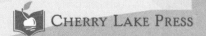

Published in the United States of America by Cherry Lake Publishing Group
Ann Arbor, Michigan
www.cherrylakepublishing.com

Reading Adviser: Beth Walker Gambro, MS, Ed., Reading Consultant, Yorkville, IL
Book Design: Jennifer Wahi
Illustrator: Jeff Bane

Photo Credits: © Amanita Silvicora/Shuttershock.com 2, 3, 24; © Dave Bromley/Shuttershock.com, 5; © Jim David/Shuttershock.com, 7; © Oleg Znamenskiy/Shuttershock.com, 9; © Johnny Coate/Shuttershock.com, 11; © leungchopan/Shuttershock.com, 13; © Susan E. Viera/Shuttershock.com, 15; © You Touch Pix of EuToch/Shuttershock.com, 17; © Svetla Ilieva/Shuttershock.com, 19; © Henri Martin/Shuttershock.com, 21; © CherylRamalho/Shuttershock.com, 23; Cover, 10, 16, 22, Jeff Bane

Cherry Lake Press is an imprint of Cherry Lake Publishing Group.

Library of Congress Cataloging-in-Publication Data

Names: Gray, Susan Heinrichs, author. | Bane, Jeff, 1957- illustrator.
Title: Desert / Susan H. Gray ; illustrated by Jeff Bane.
Description: Ann Arbor, Michigan : Cherry Lake Publishing, 2022. | Series: My guide to earth's habitats | Audience: Grades K-1
Identifiers: LCCN 2022005312 | ISBN 9781668910580 (paperback) | ISBN 9781668908983 (hardcover) | ISBN 9781668912171 (ebook) | ISBN 9781668913765 (pdf)
Subjects: LCSH: Desert ecology--Juvenile literature. | Deserts--Juvenile literature.
Classification: LCC QH541.5.D4 G729 2022 | DDC 577.54--dc23/eng/20220214
LC record available at https://lccn.loc.gov/2022005312

Printed in the United States of America

About the author: Susan H. Gray has a master's degree in zoology. She loves writing science books, especially about animals. Susan lives in Arkansas with her husband, Michael. She prefers not to live in a desert.

About the illustrator: Jeff Bane and his two business partners own a studio along the American River in Folsom, California, home of the 1849 Gold Rush. When Jeff's not sketching or illustrating for clients, he's either swimming or kayaking in the river to relax.

What is a desert? It is a dry, dry land. Rain is **rare**.

Some deserts are hot.
Others are very cold.
Some are both.

What lives in deserts? Plants and animals do! They know how to **survive**.

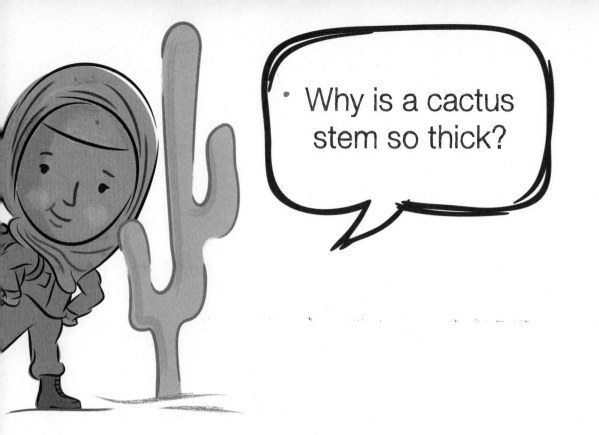

Why is a cactus stem so thick?

The plants store water. A **cactus** stores it in its stem.

Some plants have **spines**. They protect the plants. Most animals **avoid** them.

Desert animals need little water. They get it from their food. Elf owls eat crickets. Cactus **wrens** eat beetles.

Why is a burrow cool?

Animals avoid the heat. Gophers hide in **burrows**. So do kangaroo rats. They stay cool there.

Some animals are built for desert life. Camels have long eyelashes. They keep dust out.

Some foxes have big ears.
The ears let off extra heat.

Desert life is not easy. But living things survive there.

glossary

avoid (uh-VOYD) to stay away from

burrows (BUHR-ohz) holes or tunnels in the ground, often used for shelter

cactus (KAK-tuhs) a plant with thick, spiny stems

rare (REHR) unusual; not happening very often

spines (SPYNZ) thin, sharp points growing from a plant or animal

survive (suhr-VYV) to continue to live

wrens (RENZ) certain small birds with brown feathers

index